THE TIGER FAMILY

TIGER I * PORSCHE-TIGER, ELEPHANT PURSUIT TANK (Ferdinand)

TIGER II (King Tiger) * HUNTING TIGER * STORM TIGER

by Horst Scheibert

Schiffer Publishing Ltd

1469 Morstein Road, West Chester, Pennsylvania 19380

Key to cover picture

1. Three fuel tanks
2. Exhaust
3. Fuel fillers
4. Ventilator
5. Air intake grille
6. Air cooler for the motor
7. Armored motor cowling
8. Turret (production turret)
9. Commander's seat
10. Commander's cupola
11. Gunner's seat (left), loader's seat (right)
12. 8.8-cm KwK L

13. Coaxial MG 34 machine gun
14. Ventilator
15. Rifling in gun barrel
16. Driver's visor
17. Shock absorber
18. Driver's seat
19. Headrest for the radioman (machine-gunner)
20. Gearbox
21. Bullet shield for MG 34
22. Six 8.8-cm cartridges
23. Radioman's seat

Photo credits:
Federal Archives, Koblenz (BA)
Photo Archives of Prussian Culture (BPK)
Library of History of the Times, Stuttgart (BfZ)
Nowarra Archives (N)
Podzun Archives
Scheibert Archives
Schröder Archives (S)

Translated from the German by Dr. Edward Force.

Copyright © 1989 by Schiffer Publishing Ltd.
Library of Congress Catalog Number: 89-084178.

Printed in the United States of America.
ISBN: 0-88740-187-2

Turkish officers examine a Tiger I on the eastern front in 1943. (BA)

The Tiger Family

Originally only a heavy armored vehicle was foreseen as the Armored Battle Vehicle IV, developed and completed in peacetime. But when the experimental models (VK) developed by the Porsche and Henschel firms far exceeded the maximum weight of 40 tons specified by the military authorities, the firms of Daimler-Benz and MAN were given new orders for a tank of this weight with the designation "Panther". But since a stronger patrol tank had been requested meanwhile, because of the powerful new Russian tanks, the experimental models (VK) 4501 (P)orsche and (H)enschel were developed further. While the Panther was given the designation of Armored Vehicle V, those developed from the VK became Armored Vehicle VI and were named Tiger.

In a comparison test, the Henschel development proved to be the better one and was now manufactured in large numbers (1,355) as Tiger (I).

But since components of the VK 4501 (P) development were already available, lesser numbers of these were produced as the Porsche-Tiger (10) and Pursuit Tank (Ferdinand) Elefant (90).

Above:
Tunis, 1943. The photo shows well the weight and power of a Tiger, but also the many vertical armored walls. From the canisters mounted on the sides of the turret, smoke bombs could be fired in time of danger to conceal withdrawal movements (BA).

Since the Tiger (I), because of its vertical, angular walls, proved to be deficient in deflecting fire, a more elegant version of it was developed. It featured not only more angled armor plates, but also a longer cannon (L/70 instead of L/56) and, a somewhat stronger armoring overall. As a result, this vehicle weighed 70 tons, as opposed to the barely 60 of Tiger I.

There were two versions of it:
—Tiger II (King Tiger) with Porsche turret (50 made), and
—Tiger II (King Tiger) with production turret by Krupp (437 made).

Toward the end of the war, as enemy tanks appeared on the battlefield in ever-greater numbers, there arose—along with numerous antitank improvisations (see Volume 2 of this series) very heavily armored pursuit tanks on the chassis of Armored Vehicles 38 (t) and IV through VI. They differed from the conventional tanks in that they lacked a turning turret and, in part, carried even heavier guns than the battle tanks. These guns were always built into the bow of the vehicle! There were two types of the Tiger version:
—Hunting Tiger with Henschel chassis, and
—Hunting Tiger with Porsche chassis (70 made in all).

Something completely new and never before appearing in this series was, finally, a
—Storm Tiger (18 made).

In this volume we provide illustrations of all the Tiger family types named above, but we have made sure that there is no repetition of earlier pictures—including those that were shown in the out-of-print volumes.

Above:
SS Hauptsturmführer Wittmann with his team, which shot down 88 tanks. They belonged to the SS Armored Division "Leibstandarte Adolf Hitler (LAH)", and were probably the most successful tank crew in World War II (N).

Battle Tank Tiger (I) Sd.Kfz. 181

The parentheses were placed around the "I" because a Tiger II (King Tiger) was not originally planned, and the number was applied only in retrospect. But it is also referred to as Tiger, Type E, as opposed to Tiger, Type B (Tiger II). In recent years, though, it has become customary to use just the Tiger I and II designations.

The Tiger I tanks built as of 1944 had new-type road wheels of steel. These replaced the disc wheels with hard rubber flanges used until then, which had only a very short lifespan. But the main reason for this change was the lack of rubber.

There were also the following versions of Tiger I:
—Armored Command Car Tiger I, and
—Armored Recovery Vehicle Tiger I.
The former can be recognized by an additional umbrella antenna, the latter by a turret, set at "6 o'clock", without a cannon.

Upper right:
Battle drill, France, 1944 (BA).
Right:
On a French practice field, spring 1944—
before the invasion (BA).

Left:
Russia, winter 43/44.
Tigers in action near
Tscherkassy. The distance
between the individual
Armored Vehicle VI units
was at least 100 meters,
usually more (BA).

Right:
A photo from the same
attack as above. In both
photos the characteristic
storage box on the back of
the Tiger's turret is
recognizable.

The name and knight's emblem on the bow of this Tiger I are noteworthy.

Loading ammunition in winter; empty shells lie on the ground.

Contrasts: On the way to the invasion front, summer 1944—Northern France (BA).

Left: After inspection. Auxiliary equipment, supplies and maintenance gear are stowed again (BfZ).

Lower left: Then comes the loading of ammunition—92 rounds could be carried in the brackets—here directly from an ammunition truck (BfZ).

Above: A later turret version, recognizable by the reinforcements around both viewing ports of the optic to the right of the cannon (BfZ).

Tunisia, 1943. A Tiger of Tiger Unit 501 interests the Tunisians. The cannon bears score rings toward the front (BA).

Above:
When looking at this photo, one can hear the deep rumbling of the three tractors that are towing a Tiger I up a slope in Tunisia (BA).

Right:
It was a lot more reassuring to march with Tigers nearby (BfZ).

Above: A Tiger I with steel road wheels. They were used on the later Tiger I (and II) because of a shortage of rubber.

Above:
A Tiger I armored command car, recognizable by the umbrella antenna.

The commander—as the Roman numeral I on the turret shows him to be—uses hand signals to show that he is ready to receive. He wears headphones in the usual position (only one earphone on the ear), so as to be able to hear not only the report but also the battle noise, necessary for judging the situation (BfZ).

Right:
A Tiger recovery vehicle. This was a Tiger without a cannon, with the turret fixed at "6 o'clock" and added winches, crane and auxiliary equipment.

Battle Tank Porsche-Tiger

It is also known by the name "Ferdinand-Tiger" after the first name of its builder.

After the Henschel-Tiger (the subsequent Tiger I) was chosen, ten Porsche-Tigers—as originally planned—were assembled out of newly produced, already available components, with Hitler's approval, and 90 "Ferdinand" pursuit tanks, later also called "Elefant", were built.

The cannon of the Porsche-Tiger was the same as used on the Tiger I made by Henschel, the turret was similar, but somewhat lower. On the basis of its powerplant (gasoline-electric), running gear and steering, this Tiger was certainly very interesting technically, but too difficult in terms of production technology and too complicated in terms of operation. For this reason, most of them were put out of action by technical failure and not by enemy action.

The two photos at right show the Porsche-Tiger during a demonstration for Hitler in Rastenburg, East Prussia, in 1942.

Pursuit Tank Tiger (P) Elefant

Sd.Kfz. 184

This was also based on the Tiger development by Porsche, the VK 4501 (P). Originally named the "Ferdinand" pursuit tank, after Porsche's first name, it was later given the official designation above. Today the following names are in use:

Pursuit Tank Porsche "Elefant" or just Pursuit Tank "Elefant".

It consisted of the complicated Porsche chassis, but unlike the Porsche-Tiger it had two Maybach HL 120 motors. Like all pursuit tanks, it did not have a turning turret, but instead a rather high superstructure, which was later equipped with a cupola. Its cannon was the longer 8.8-cm Pak 43/2 L/71 also used in the Tiger II (The Tiger I had only the 8.8-cm L/56).

The vehicle was not very mobile and was used since 1943 in heavy tank destroyer units—mostly in Italy, less often in Russia. As with all products made in small numbers, it suffered from a shortage of spare parts, and within the units there were cases of "cannibalism", when out-of-service vehicles were stripped to keep others in action. For this reason, and because of its general mechanical difficulties, the "Elephants" were put out of action more by technical problems than by enemy action.

Like the Porsche-Tiger, it was not perfected, too complicated and thus a practical failure.

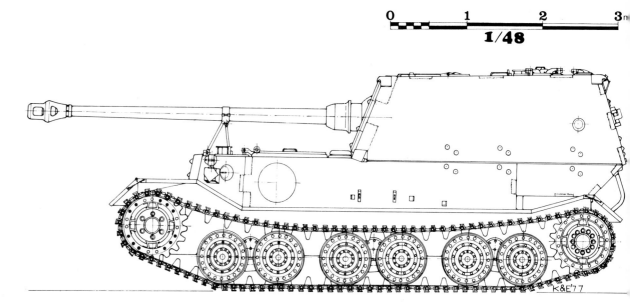

1/48

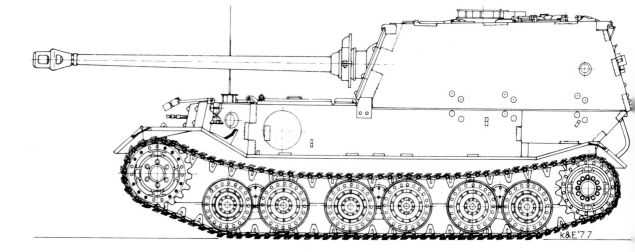

The two drawings show the earlier (above, without bow machine gun) and later (below, with panoramic cupola) versions.

This version does not have a machine gun at the bow, but does have the protective shield around the gun-barrel before the opening.

An "Elefant" pursuit tank, without a machine gun in the loophole, but partly covered with Zimmerite. These tanks were armored up to 200 mm.

All three photos come from Operation "Citadel", the battle around Kursk. They show Russian soldiers examining abandoned "Elefant" pursuit tanks after the German withdrawal. These are vehicles of the heavy tank destroyer unit 665. They presumably broke down for technical reasons.

Upper left:
The Inspector-General of the armored troops, Senior General Guderian, observes a Ferdinand unit's shooting practice through a scissor telescope in 1943 (BPK).

Above:
This "Elefant" was destroyed in Sariano, Italy. It is the same pursuit tank shown on the next page.

Left: An "Elefant" under eucalyptus trees in Italy (BA).

Above: This "Elefant" was presumably blown up during a withdrawal and thrown on its side in the process.

Upper right:
Here is another view of the tank in Soriano.

Right: A direct front view.

This picture of the "Elefant" pursuit tank shows clearly
the length of the cannon, but also the height of the body
and its angular form.

Above: Completely new Tiger (P) "Elefant" pursuit tanks, Sd. Kfz. 184, roll out of the factory. They have not yet been painted in camouflage colors or had Zimmerite applied.

On the opposite page are four more pictures of this complicated pursuit tank, of which only 90 were made.

Upper left:
The front view of a Tiger (P) pursuit tank without a bow machine gun or the round gun-cradle apron (hatch protector) around the gun barrel.

Above:
This tank also shows the earlier version, which was often called "Ferdinand" instead of "Elefant". This was not official, for when the name "Elefant" was chosen, it was also applied to the earlier products.

Left:
An abandoned "Elefant" at a roadside. It shows the two signs of the later version.

Battle Tank Tiger II (King Tiger) Sd.Kfz. 182

with Porsche Turret

There were two reasons that led to the production of the Tiger II battle tank. First, the angular form of the Tiger I proved to be disadvantageous; second, the Weapons Office had ordered the firms of Henschel (Tiger) and MAN (Panther) to carry out a thorough-going assimilation of their tanks. Both firms developed new designs for this purpose. While that of the "Panther II" never went into production, the Tiger II appeared quite soon. It was called "King Tiger" by the Allies, a name that the German side also accepted later. It no longer had the vertical armored walls of the Tiger I, and was given a longer cannon (L/71).

As already mentioned, a shot-deflecting turret was developed for the Porsche-Tiger, and 50 examples were built. But since the Porsche-Tiger was no longer produced, for reasons already stated, the first 50 King Tigers were fitted with these turrets, which were equipped with roller blinds. The later turrets were made by the firm of Krupp, were called production turrets, and were recognizable by their simplifications (narrower and without a roller blind). Even so, 85 shells (instead of 78 in the Porsche turret) could be carried.

Other versions of it were an
—Armored Command Tank Tiger II, and an
—Armored Recovery Vehicle Tiger II.
Both resembled the corresponding versions of the Tiger I.

Right:
A Tiger II with Porsche turret (recognizable by its rounded front) drives through the washing area.

This photo shows the clean lines of the Tiger II—similar to those of the Panther and resembling the T-34 (BA).

Here the width (almost four meters) is easy to see.

Battle Tank Tiger II (King Tiger) Sd.Kfz. 182

with production turret

Left page:
A Tiger II with the production turret made by Krupp. It shows Zimmerite covering and hooks on the turret to hold spare track links (BA).

Below:
Technical service for a Tank VI/II (BA).

Above:
A King Tiger in Budapest, 1944 (BA).

This picture makes details of the Krupp turret easy to identify. At right front is the driver, at left the radioman and bow machine-gunner (BA).

Pursuit Tank Hunting Tiger, Type B Sd.Kfz. 186

Following a tendency of the last war years, there was also a version of Armored Battle Tank VI as a pursuit tank. It was called the "Hunting Tiger" and, like all pursuit tanks, did not have a rotating turret—and was heavily armored. Its armament was the 12.8-cm Pak. With its high weight of around 76 tons and this large-caliber gun, it was the heaviest and strongest tank that saw service in the German Army. Thus it was superior to all other tanks of the time.

This superiority was not fully utilized, though, since it could be built only in small (70) numbers and, because of its weight, had a very unfavorable power-to-weight ratio of only 8 HP per ton. It was also too unmaneuverable off the road, often got stuck in unknown country, and then had to be abandoned, as towing on the battlefield at a time when the German troops had to retreat was usually impossible.

There were two different versions of it; they differed in terms of their running gear. Most of them had the box-type running gear made by Henschel, with nine road wheels on each side. The others had the sprung roller type made by Porsche, with eight road wheels on each side.

Below:
The upper drawing shows the Hunting Tiger with the Porsche running gear, the lower one with the Henschel running gear.

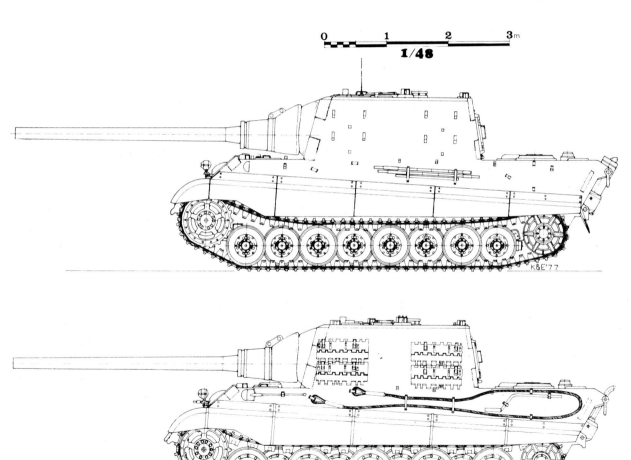

1/48

Here is a Hunting Tiger without camouflage paint, Zimmerite covering or outer equipment (BA).

A Hunting Tiger with the Porsche running gear. Its height was almost three meters, its strongest armor 200 mm (S).

The three photos on this page do not show whether the Hunting Tiger pursuit tanks shown in them have the Henschel or Porsche running gear (1 x S, 1 x N).

This Hunting Tiger stopped in a West German town shortly before the end of the war. It shows its mighty dimensions in comparison to the Jeep.

All three photos show Hunting Tigers with the Porsche running gear, consisting of eight road wheels.

In the two upper photos it can be seen that it had been given a Zimmerite covering only as high as a soldier could reach. The Hunting Tiger shown in this photo was lost in France and is being towed away by Allied vehicles here.

The photo at left was taken on the proving ground of the Nibelungenwerke, at which all Hunting Tigers were produced.

Hunting Tigers with the Henschel running gear can be seen in these three pictures.

The two upper photos show a Hunting Tiger that was destroyed in France.

The right photo is another picture of the Hunting Tiger shown two pages before (N).

On these two pages destroyed Hunting Tigers can be seen. They were taken, except for the upper left photo, in central Germany (for example, in the Harz), where Hunting Tigers were last used.

Whether the situation in the upper left photo resulted from a direct hit that caused the ammunition to explode, or an ordered explosion, is hard to say.

Accompanying Tank
Storm Tiger

The desire to support attacking infantry directly with quickly mobile howitzers led to the development of accompanying or "storming" tanks. The first was a storming gun on the chassis of armored vehicle III, already used in the French campaign but then, for reasons of urgency, changed to a tank destroyer. But again and again in the last years of the war, genuine accompanying tanks appeared on the battlefield. They are recognizable by their usually large-caliber howitzers, as opposed to the long guns of the pursuit tanks.

An exception of sorts was the Storm Tiger accompanying tank, since it carried not the planned (but not available in time) 21-cm howitzer, but the 38-cm caliber RW 61 rocket launcher. This launcher had been developed by the Rheinmetall firm, originally for anti-submarine use.

The Storm Tiger served excellently in attacking individual short-range targets under heavy fire. The designation of "storming mortar", which is also found, is inexact, for though it gave the external appearance of a mortar, its ammunition was rockets.

These consisted of two parts, the propelling charge and the explosive charge. They existed in the form of explosive shells and hollow charges. Their maximum range was about 6000 meters, and their effect on a target was crippling.

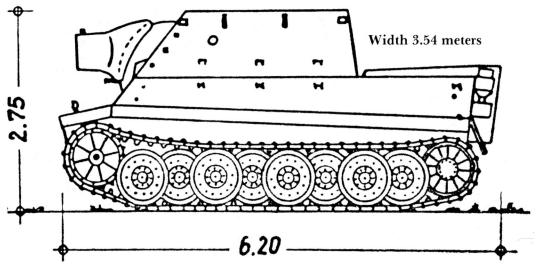

Width 3.54 meters

2.75

6.20

Eighteen of these tanks were produced by the firm of Alkett in Berlin. For them the firm utilized Tiger-I chassis of the later type (see the running gear with steel wheels), and equipped them with boxy bodies, as well as some additional bow armor. Of the eighteen, about ten were used in the East (first action in August of 1944) and later in the Eifel, the Ardennes offensive, and finally in the Ruhr Basin.

Above:
The fighting compartment is farther forward than in the Hunting Tiger.

Its height of 2.46 meters is less than that of the Hunting Tiger and "Elefant" pursuit tank; the running gear is made by Porsche (N).

Right page:
A rare photo: A prototype with a somewhat different launcher (no cams on the tube) and the older Tiger running gear (BA).

Above: Here a prototype of the Storm Tiger is displayed to Hitler (October 20, 1943). The gas exhaust holes between the inner casing and outer mantle of the launcher are smaller and fewer in number. It also has extra bow armor riveted on. The size of the storming tank can be seen clearly in comparison to Hitler and his companions (N).

On this page a later model is shown, which stands today
(with false camouflage paint) in an American open-air
museum. It also has a different (the final) shield to protect
the union of barrel and mentlet (N).

The two upper photos are the same photo. At left is the actual photograph, in which American soldiers examine a captured Storm Tiger and its ammunition. In the right picture, the tree and soldiers have been retouched out.

In the photo at left, the usual stern of the Tiger is clearly recognizable. It is also easy to see that almost all the Storm Tigers used the later Tiger chassis—with steel wheels.

The device on the superstructure is a crane used to move the rockets into their holders in the fighting compartment or to load the launcher (front loader!) (S).

Above:
Here again the holes between the inner casing and barrel mantle can be seen clearly; it was their job to direct the excess exhaust gases out to the front.

Upper right:
This picture shows the launcher at its highest elevation. It can be seen here that the barrel and protective shield consist of a single piece. The launcher was loaded in this position.

Right:
This picture effectively captures the bullish form of the Storm Tiger.

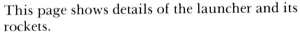

This page shows details of the launcher and its rockets.

Its massive form can be seen above. The soldier's finger shows the joint of the explosive (above) and propelling charges.

At the upper right the opened base of the launcher can be seen. From here the propelling charge was loaded, while the explosive shell was added from outside.

The photo at the lower right shows the lower part of the propelling charge with the detonator (hand).

The Storm Tiger could carry thirteen rockets, six inside, on either side of the fighting compartment, and one in the launcher.

Technical Data

Tiger II (King Tiger)

Motor	Carbureted 25-liter Maybach HL 230 P 45
Cylinders	V-12 60-degree
Bore x stroke	130 x 145 mm
Displacement	23,880 cc
Highest power	700 HP at 3000 rpm
Sustained power	600 HP at 2500 rpm
Compression	1 : 6.8
Carburetors	4 Solex 52 JFF II D double downdraft all-terrain
Valves	Dropped, 1 gear-driven camshaft per cylinder head
Crankshaft	8-bearing, changeable cylinder liners
Cooling	Water-cooled by pump
Battery	2 120 volt 150 Ah.
Generator	1000 W
Starter	6 HP
Transmission	Rear motor, chain drive, semi-automatic pre-selector gearbox
Gears	Maybach Olvar 40 12 16, 8 forward speeds, 4 reverse
Drive ratio	Lateral, 10.7
Chassis & body	Self-supporting armored hull, armored body with rotating turret, powered by vehicle motor
Tracks	2 tracks of 96 130-mm links each, front drive, rear steering, 9 pairs of staggered road wheels, 2 springs per pair of wheels
Steering	Hydraulic two-wheel steering controlled by steering wheel
Brakes	Drive wheels have Argus hydraulic disc brakes

General data:

Track	2790 mm, with shipping tracks 2610 mm
Track width	800 mm, shipping tracks 600 mm
Dimensions	7260 x 3625 x 3090 mm, with gun & aprons: 10286 x 3755 x 3090 mm; overall shipping width 3270 mm
Armor	Front 100 to 185 mm, sides & rear 80 mm
Ground clearance	485 mm
Fording ability	1600 mm
Turning circle	5 meters
Gross weight	68.000 kg
Top speed	40 kph
Fuel consumption	Road 680
Cross-country	1000 liters/100 km
Fuel capacity	860 liters (7 tanks)
Range	Road 120, cross-country 80 km
Crew	5 men
Armament	8.8-cm KwK 43 L/71 & 2 machine guns

Pursuit Tank Elefant

Motors	2 Maybach HL 120 TRM carbureted motors
Cylinders	2 V-12 60-degree motors
Bore x stroke	106 x 115 mm
Displacement	2 x 11,867 cc
Highest power	2 x 320 HP at 2800 rpm
Sustained power	2 x 265 HP at 2600 rpm
Compression	1 : 6.5
Carburetors	2 x 2 Solex 40 JFF II double downdraft cross-country
Valves	Dropped, 1 gear-driven camshaft per cylinder head
Crankshafts	2 x 7 bearings, changeable cylinder liners
Cooling	Water-cooled by pump
Batteries	2 x 12-volt 120 Ah.
Generators	2 x 600 W
Starters	2 x 4 HP
Transmission	2 rear engines, gasoline-electric chain drive, made by Porsche/Siemens Schuckert
Gears	3 forward speeds
Drive ratios	total 16.75
Chassis & body	Self-supporting armored hull, armored body without rotating turret
Tracks	2 tracks of 109 links each, front drive, rear steering, 8 pairs of road wheels in line, two springs per pair of wheels
Steering/brakes	Hydropneumatic steering brakes

General data:

Track	2680 mm
Track width	650 mm
Dimensions	6800 x 3430 x 2970 mm; with gun 8140 x 3430 x 2970 mm
Armor	Front 200 mm, sides & rear 80 mm
Ground clearance	480 mm
Wading ability	1000 mm
Turning circle	2.5 meters
Gross weight	68,000 kg
Fuel consumption	Road 700, cross-country 1000 liters per 100 km
Fuel capacity	950 liters
Range	Road 130, cross-country 90 km
Crew	6 men
Armament	8.8-cm Pak 43/2 L/71 & 1 machine gun (at first unmounted, later bow-mounted)

Storm Tiger

Length	6.31 meters
Width	3.73 meters
Height	3.46 meters
Gross weight	68 tons
Crew	5 men
Armor, front	100 (140) mm
Armor, sides	60 mm
Armor, rear	85 mm (hull)

Fighting compart-ment armor

	front 100, sides & top 40 mm
Armament	1 each 38-mm rocket launcher 61, 7.92 MG 34
Motor	Maybach V12
Power	700 HP at 300 rpm
Transmission	Olvar 40 12 16, 8 forward speeds, 4 reverse

47

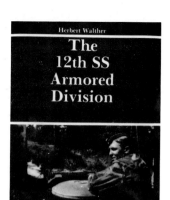
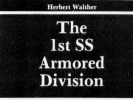
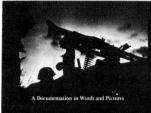

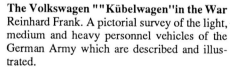